Writing Your Peace

365 Writing Prompts for Coping with Grief, Loss, Life, and Relationships.

By

Janele Nicole

©2018. Janele Nicole (USA).

This edition published by Janele Nicole (USA).

All rights reserved. No part of this publication may be reproduced, stored, or transmitted in any form or by any means, electronic, photocopied, recording, mechanical, or otherwise, without consent of the publisher.

10 9 8 7 6 5 4 3 2 1

Printed in the USA

ISBN-13: **978-0-692-09243-9**

THE INTRODUCTION

"SOMETIMES YOU DON'T REALIZE YOUR OWN STRENGTH UNTIL YOU COME FACE TO FACE WITH YOUR GREATEST WEAKNESS"- SUSAN GALE

On December 15, 1997, I lost my mother to Lupus. She has battled with the illness since she was sixteen years old. She was only thirty-four years of age when she passed away.

At the time, I was only six years old. The memories that I have of my mom are very vague. Sometimes I wish that I could revisit the past just to hear her voice. I can't remember the way she sounds. My family tells me so many stories about my mother, all good things. She was a woman with a big heart and I am always glad to hear someone say that I am the spitting image of her or that I embody her mind, body, and soul. She was nothing short of amazing; an earth angel.

In losing my mom, I found a love in writing. When I was younger, I would write letters to my mother in heaven, prayer notes to God, short poems, songs, and journal entries. Writing became an escape for me. I love words because they are very powerful. I love to inspire and make people feel good in reading my material.

Do you know the saying "sticks and stones may break your bones, but words will never hurt you"? I don't believe that to be true. If I could rephrase it, it would be "sticks and stone may leave a bruise, but words leave mental wounds".

With that in mind, I have created this writing prompt journal as an escape for anybody who is looking for productive ways to deal with mental pain. Mental pain can be any form of depression. Coping with grief, loss, relationships, self-esteem, and self-confidence issues.

This journal is designed to help manage these issues one day at a time. Writing helps to release built up energy in ways that are positive. Making a daily habit of writing is helpful to making a healthier daily change in your life. I hope that everyone can enjoy this journal and enjoy writing as much as I do. So, on your mark, get set, drop the pen to the paper, and tell your story!!

WRITE FEARLESSLY!!!

THIS JOURNAL BELONGS TO

───────────────────────────────────────

I

Grief and Loss

"In life, all losses are never a true loss, but a win after the smoke has cleared. We go through loss to gain strength for the win."- Chris Bishop (High Klass Hair)

1. Write a letter to someone close to you that has passed away. Use these prompts to help you.

My happiest memory of you…
I remember when…
I've always wanted to tell you…
The greatest lesson I have learned….

_____
_____
_____
_____
_____
_____
_____
_____
_____
_____
_____
_____
_____
_____
_____
_____
_____
_____
_____
_____
_____
_____
_____
_____
_____
_____
_____
_____
_____
_____

2. Write about your pain or sorrow for 10 minutes WITHOUT stopping. Let your thoughts go, let the tears flow! This is the cleansing process.

3. Make a list of things that unexpectedly happened in your life.

4. How did those things change your life?

5. Have you learned or grown from the situation(s)?

6. If those things didn't happen, do you think you would be the person that you are today?

7. If you could change one thing from your list, what would it be? Why?

8. What is a priority for you right now?

9. Think of one word that sums up how you feel today. Why'd you choose that word?

10. Write what you loved or remembered most about your lost loved ones:
   Touch...
   Smell...
   Looks...
   Personality...

11. How do you feel after bringing up those memories?

12. What brings you the most joy about your lost loved one?

13. What makes you feel peaceful concerning your lost loved one?

14. What do you think about when you fall asleep?

15. Think of some ways your lost loved one influenced you?

16. What days, activities, songs, smells, or movies recreate your acute grief?

17. How do you think your loved one would want to be remembered?

18. What is one thing you would say that others feel that you and your loved one have in common?

19. Did you experience shock of a loss for words when your loved one passed? Or did you instantly react to the news?

20. Where were you when you received the news?

21. What is one thing that you do that helps you cope with grief daily?

22. Do you believe in GOD?

23. Name one drastic change that has occurred since losing your loved one?

24. How did the loss of a loved one mentally change you?

25. Do you believe you went through/going through any mental challenges in the event of losing someone?

26. Have you ever experienced survivor's guilt/survivor's remorse?

27. After your loved one died, did you feel like you could no longer go on?

28. Do you feel guilty about your loved one passing?

29. Write a "goodbye" letter to your lost loved one.

30. Is there anything that you've always wanted to tell your loved one, but didn't?

31. Is there anything that you want to tell your family about your loss? Immediate family that experienced the loss with you?

32. Who do you talk to the most about your lost loved one?

33. Write a conversation with your loved one. Imagine what they would say in the conversation.

34. What did some friends or family do that was helpful to you during your tough times?

35. Write the story of your loved one's passing in your own words of how YOU remember it.

36. What was life like for you before the passing of your loved one?

37. Are you angry about the loss of your loved one?

38. Do you often mask your feelings?

39. Do you often think that others may judge you if you express certain feelings?

40. Do you feel responsible for the death of your loved one in some way?

41. What are some things that people say to you while you're grieving; that you wish they'd stop saying?

42. Have you ever denied help after losing a loved one when you really needed/wanted help?

43. Do you think your lost loved one ever came to you in a dream?

44. Do you still feel the presence of your loved one?

45. At what point do you feel like you first begin your grieving process?

46. Do you ever say that you're okay when you aren't, if someone were to ask you about your loved one?

47. Have you ever been told "things could be worse" or "you'll get over it" when talking to someone about the death of a loved one?

48. How does it make you feel when people say things like that?

49. Have you ever lost a fur baby (pet)? If not, how do you think you would feel if you did?

50. How did/are you coping with the loss of your fur baby?

51. Do you feel like you haven't been able to fulfill a major dream of yours?

52. What is one dream that you've always wanted to fulfill, but you feel like it cannot be reached now? Why?

53. Are you or anyone that you're close with battling mental illness?

54. In what ways has the mental illness affected you?

55. Do you feel like you lost a loved one, in the sense of how they used to be to mental illness?

56. Do you have a loved one that suffers from a sickness or terminal illness?

57. How has their illness/sickness changed their attitude or personality?

58. After dealing with the death of a loved one, do you fear losing other loved ones that are in your life?

59. How often do you think about death and losing your loved ones that are still living?

60. How often do you tell your loved ones that you love them?

61. Do you think of your own death? If so, does it scare you?

62. How often do you express your feelings to your loved ones?

63. After experiencing the death of a loved one, what advice would you give to someone else that is experiencing a loss as well?

64. Write about a time that you had to let go of someone that you loved.

65. Have you gained awareness through your loss?

66. Do you think it would be more difficult to deal with the process of a terminal illness or a sudden death?

67. Have you ever or do you know someone who has experienced a house fire?

68. Have you ever or do you know someone that has experienced a natural disaster?

69. How were they or yourself affected by the fire?

70. In what ways were they or yourself affected by the natural disaster?

71. Have you ever thought about how your response/reaction would be to losing a specific loved one?

72. In what way is death scary to you?

73. How do you feel about the life changes that come after a loss?

74. Are you afraid that things may get worse after a loss?

75. Does it make you uncomfortable talking about how the loss has affected you?

76. How often do you think about death? Explain.

77. Have you ever dreamt your own death? Describe the dream(s).

78. Write a list of things that you've lost that you wish you still had possession of.

79. What were the most important things on your list?

80. Why are they important to you? What value did they hold?

81. Do you live out of state? Do you have family or friends that live out of state?

82. How did you feel when they left or when you moved away?

83. How long have they/you been away? Do they often come to visit? Do you visit?

84. Do you have any family members or friends incarcerated?

85. How did you feel when they were first taken away to prison?

86. How has their imprisonment affected you and your family?

87. If you could write a letter to the judge to release your loved one, what would it say?

88. Do you have any family overseas or in the armed forces?

89. How has their deployment affected you and your family?

90. How often do you get to see your loved one(s)?

91. How often do you get to talk to your loved one?

92. Have you ever lost a loved one that was serving our country?

93. How did the loss affect your loved ones, yourself, and close friends of the lost loved one?

94. Have you ever lost a job that was very important to you at the time?

95. How did losing that job affect you?

96. Explain how you felt the day you lost your job.

97. Do you see a therapist to talk about your loss and life?

98. Would you consider seeing a therapist, if you don't already?

99. Generally, how often do your loved ones, family, or friends reach out to you?

100. In what ways are you feeling differently now, as compared to the past or when you first experienced your loss?

101. In what ways have any loss that you've experienced been harder to deal with than what you expected?

102. Life insurance is very important. Do you or your family members have life insurance coverage? What was your decision in getting it?

103. Do you have any other types of insurance? Homeowner's, renters, etc.?

104. Why do you think having this coverage is important?

105. Do you believe that it is important to have a will in good standing?

106. In your words, write what you think your lost loved ones' will would have stated in the event of their passing.

107. What has helped you to stay strong in your difficult times?

108. Name the stages and types of grief that you've been through.

109. What does faith mean to you?

110. What is one thing that you're going to do differently after completing this writing prompt segment?

USE THIS PAGE TO POST PHOTOS OF YOUR GREATEST MEMORIES OF YOUR LOST LOVED ONES

Life and Relationships

"There comes a point in your life when you realize who really matters, who never did, and who always will." -Adam Lindsey Gordon

1. What makes a good friend?

2. Who is your best friend?

3. What do you love about your best friend?

4. If you could describe your best friend in one word, what would it be?

5. Would you say that you are a good friend?

6. Name three things that you could do to become a better friend. Why?

7. Are you close with your family?

8. What side of your family do you spend the most time with?

9. Describe your dad's side of your family.

10. Describe your mother's side of your family.

11. Do you have a favorite cousin? Who? Why?

12. Growing up, who took care of you?

13. Do you have any children?

14. How is your relationship with your children? If any.

15. How many children do you? How are they?

16. Has anyone ever put you in a life-threatening situation?

17. Describe the day you met your best friend.

18. Describe this day from your friends' point of view.

19. Have you ever snooped through a friends' or partners' house/items?

20. What is your favorite aspect of your partner?

21. Describe something that you admire about your best friend.

22. What is your longest friendship? What is their name?

23. Why is family so important?

24. Have you ever been in an abusive relationship?

25. Have you ever felt that you deserved any abuse that you've been subjected to?

26. No one deserves abuse and it is never the victims fault. But, have you ever felt a sense of blame in the situation?

27. Has anyone ever pointed blame on you over a situation that has put you in harm's way by hands of someone else?

28. Have you ever felt paranoid about a situation? Why?

29. How did the paranoia affect you in your daily life?

30. Who do you trust the most?

31. Who do you trust the least?

32. What is your relationship like with your mom?

33. What is your relationship like with your father?

34. Describe your relationship with God.

35. How important is loyalty to you in your relationships?

36. What are your views on marriage?

37. What are your feelings about pre-marital sex?

38. What are your views about celibacy?

39. Write about a situation of a time you felt that you've given someone majority, if not all your trust.

40. Did you feel comfortable in trusting that person/people? Explain.

41. Do you believe that you are happier in a relationship?

42. Have you ever encountered someone that has brought, what you feel, is an endless battle to your life?

43. If you could have dinner with someone from your past that's still living, who would it be? Why?

44. Do you remember your first love?

45. Do you believe that you can be with someone that you love even if you aren't deeply in love?

46. Do you believe in soulmates? Explain why.

47. Do you feel completed being in a relationship?

48. What are the relationships in your life that are taking from you?

49. How do you know when a relationship (business, friendship, etc.) needs to end?

50. When is the last time that you've taken someone or have been taken on a date?

51. Who do you look up to the most?

52. Who do you believe is in your way or holding you back? Yourself or the people around you?

53. Do you believe the people in your life accept you when you're "on" and "off" your game?

54. Do you think they treat you differently when you're "off"?

55. Do you believe that they experience a sense of contentment when you're off? If so, why?

56. How often do you show the love that you have for your loved ones?

57. Are you or have you ever been married?

58. If not, do you want to get married? If so, how long have you been married?

59. What is your marriage like? How would you want your marriage to be?

60. Do you believe that it is appropriate to hang with a friend of the opposite sex while you're in a relationship? Explain.

61. Would you be okay with your partner/spouse hanging with a friend of the opposite sex? Explain.

62. Are you comfortable around your partner's/spouse's family? Vice versa?

63. Who do you get along with the best from your partner's/spouse's family?

64. What are 5 key things that you look for in a person before building a relationship or friendship?

65. Do you believe that romantic relationships are the most meaningful elements of life?

66. How important is compromise in relationships? Explain.

69. What are the benefits of friendships? Explain.

70. How many friends do you believe is a good number to have around you?

71. How does social media affect relationships?

72. How often does your family and friends come to you for advice?

73. How often do you open up to your friends and family?

74. Explain the phrase "Think of friendships as an emotional bank account".

75. How often do you make an effort to see your family and friends?

76. In what ways do you believe your friends shape your future?

77. How do you maintain your friendships when you are going through different stages in your life?

78. Are you doing the things in life that you knew you should be doing? Explain.

79. Write the three most important aspects of each part of life in family, love, work, health, spirituality, and sex.

80. Explain your importance for each aspect.

81. Did you make any of your loved ones feel better today? If not, what can you do to make that happen?

82. What does mentorship mean to you?

83. Describe your relationship with your mentor. If you don't have one, who would you want to be your mentor and why?

84. Describe what a dream vacation for you and your friend would be like?

85. Do you share common interests with your family and friends?

86. Have you ever been with someone, said nothing, and walked away feeling like you just had the best conversation?

87. Do you know how and when your parents met?

88. What traditions have been passed down in your family?

89. Are you pressured by your friends and family to act a certain way?

90. What would you say was the saddest time for your family?

91. What was the most joyous time for your family?

92. Explain how cultural differences play a role in family structure.

93. Name a celebrity that you admire. Would you want them as a friend? Why?

94. Describe your family in three words. Why?

95. Who is the kindest person that you know?

96. Who is the smartest person in your family? Friend?

97. What do you love most about your family?

98. In relationships, do you share yourself to the same depth you are asking of the other person?

99. What kind of impact do you believe you have on others?

100. What are your views on same-sex partnership?

101. Do you have a confidante?

102. Do you have siblings? How many? Who? How old are they?

103. If not, have you ever wanted siblings? Why?

104. Describe what your relationship is like/ could be with your siblings.

105. Explain how "people pleasing" can damage relationships.

106. Explain how giving up control helps you to experience better relationships.

107. Are you accepting of meeting people and making new friends?

108. Do you have nieces and/or nephews? How is you relationship with them?

109. What advice would you give to the younger generation of your family?

110. What is one thing that you're going to do different after completing this writing prompt segment?

POST PHOTOS OF YOUR GREATEST MEMORIES WITH YOUR FAMILY AND FRIENDS HERE

Self-Healing and Self-Reflection

"Become a weapon physically, spiritually, and mentally so that you can destroy any bullshit that comes your way."- Wayno (Triangle Offense Management)

1. What brings you the most joy in life?

_____
_____
_____
_____
_____
_____
_____
_____
_____
_____
_____
_____
_____
_____
_____
_____
_____
_____
_____
_____
_____
_____
_____
_____
_____
_____
_____
_____

2. What is something you are very good at?

3. When you have extra time on your hands, what do you like to do?

4. What is the most beautiful thing about yourself?

5. What would be the perfect vacation for you?

6. What is something that you dislike about yourself? Why?

7. What makes you feel safe?

8. Name something that brings you the most peace. Why?

9. Describe three things that you would do to make your life better.

10. What are you most proud of about yourself?

11. Name a few of your talents.

12. Where is your favorite place to be in your home? Where do you spend the most time? Why?

13. What is one thing that can change your mood from good to bad instantly?

14. What are your views on suicide?

15. Have you ever attempted to commit suicide or had suicidal thoughts?

16. Many people feel as if no one cares about them. Name one person, other than yourself, that has always shown you that they care about you?

17. You are loved! Name three things that you absolutely love about yourself. Why?

18. Name a character from a movie that you can relate to the most. Why?

19. If you could apply a personality trait from that character to add to your personality, what would it be? Why?

20. In tough situations, what do you do to control your emotions so that they don't control you?

21. Finish the sentence: When I am angry...

22. Increasing your mental strength isn't about suppressing your emotions. Explain a way that you can develop mental strength.

23. What is your favorite time of the day? Why?

24. If you could talk to your teenage self, what would you say?

25. Do you love yourself unconditionally?

26. What do you love most about your life?

27. Describe yourself using only 10 words.

28. Make a list of the things that inspire you.

29. Make a list of things that you've always wanted to or will say "NO" to.

30. Make a list of some of the things that you will say "YES" to with no hesitation.

31. What have/can you learn from your biggest mistakes?

32. If your body could talk, what would it say to you?

33. What is one thing that you wish your loved ones knew about you?

34. Would you ever be comfortable telling them?

35. What is one thing that you can't live without?

36. What are your views on money?

37. If you had $500,000 how would you spend it?

38. Do you like luxury designer brands?

39. What holds more value to you; family or money? Explain.

40. Do you think that money can save the world? Why?

41. Do you think that money makes people better?

42. Does money buy happiness?

43. Do you pray? How often?

44. Do you or have you ever meditated?

45. If so, how does meditation make you feel? If not, do you think it can help you in your daily life?

46. Is there a mistake/bad choice that you keep making in your life, repeatedly?

47. What is a priority for you right now?

48. In what way are you making the world a better place?

49. What do you think you are destined to be in this life?

50. What do you want most out of life: happiness or success? Explain.

51. When was the last time you truly listened to someone?

52. What type/genre of music would describe your mind? Why?

53. How well do you budget?

54. When do you feel the most loved?

55. What are some of your good habits?

56. What are some of your bad habits?

57. Do you believe that you're in control of your own destiny?

58. What do you think your purpose is in life?

59. What do you believe is one of the most valuable gifts that you can give yourself?

60. Do you ever feel like you are unworthy of love or belonging?

61. Has shame ever damaged you?

62. What does shame mean to you?

63. Do you practice compassion?

64. Do you feel like God is always available for you?

65. What have you learned about vulnerability?

66. Do you believe that you're an open-hearted or whole-hearted person? Why?

67. Explain the difference between the two.

68. What is your greatest accomplishment to date?

69. What has been the most complex roadblock in life for you?

70. Do you feel like you have overcome it? Is it still a major hurdle for you?

71. What do you think it will take to overcome it? Did you overcome it?

72. Do you have the desire to re-evaluate your position in the present to gain momentum for the future?

73. How often do you find yourself trying to change the mindset of others?

74. What is your greatest fear in life?

75. Would you ever consider re-locating? Why would you do so?

76. Where would you relocate your life? Why do you feel that would be the best move for you?

77. What are some childhood moments that's had an impact on how you live today?

78. What are some moments from adulthood that have made an impact on how you live today?

79. How many opportunities that were beneficial that you've turned away because you weren't as open and accepting to the possibilities?

80. If you could live to see any event in the future, what would it be?

81. What do you believe are some of the hardest facts of life?

82. What do you think the worst emotion that anyone can feel is?

83. What is the most beautiful thing in the world, in your eyes?

84. If you could spend any amount of time on a movie set, which would it be? Why?

85. In one way, explain how you do not fit in with the family that you grew up in.

86. Describe your life in three chapters, past to present, and give each segment a title.

87. Do you like your name? Why? If not, what would you change it to? Why?

88. Complete the thought: I will never...

89. What is the most important lesson that you've learned from the mistakes in your life?

90. Do you believe that it is better to be impetuous or cautious?

91. What do you think is the root of depression?

92. How much time do you spend on self-care?

93. How often do you exercise?

94. How are your eating habits?

95. What do you believe is that greatest danger that we face in life?

96. What is your view on reality?

97. Do you think they see people as they are or as you think they could/should be?

98. When you look into the mirror, what do you see?

99. If you could be doing anything in the world, what would it be?

100. Does your pride prevent you from apologizing and making necessary amends?

101. Do you know how to swim?

102. What do you think is a flaw that you possess that others see in you that you may not?

103. Are you becoming the person that you want to be?

104. In your words, explain what it means to be lonely vs. being alone.

105. What is the last thing that you've done to "perfect" yourself?

106. Describe what you were like as a child or preteen.

107. Who is in your top ten call list?

108. Do you have any mentors in life? Who are they?

109. Are you giving them the attention that you want given to you?

110. What is one thing that you're going to do differently after completing this writing prompt segment?

USE THIS PAGE TO POST YOUR FAVORITE PHOTOS OF YOURSELF (FROM CHILD TO ADULT)

Perhaps, a Date!

"To be yourself in a world that is constantly trying to make you something else is the greatest accomplishment". –Ralph Waldo Emerson

1. Who are you?
___

2. What would you say you are most passionate about?

3. What are your values?

4. What do you represent?

5. What do you want to embody?

6. Do you truly love yourself?

7. What is your ideal self? Explain.

8. Are you living the life of your dreams?

9. What does it mean to be your highest self?

10. What would you do if you could not fail?

11. How important are your goals to you?

12. Are you putting any part of your life on hold? Why?

13. Is there anything that you are running away from?

14. Are you settling for less than what you are worth?

15. Where are you living mentally? Past, present, or future? Explain.

16. How can you make your life more meaningful?

17. What are the people like that you spend the most time with?

18. Who inspires you the most?

19. In what ways would you like to be more like them?

20. What does life mean to you?

21. Name ten good habits that you cultivate.

22. Name ten bad habits that you wish to change.

23. What would you have to say to yourself in one year?

24. If you could eat one thing, every day for the rest of your life, what would it be? Why?

25. What would you say your favorite color is? Why?

26. What are your nicknames? If any.

27. What type of material do you like to read? Why?

28. What type of music do you often listen to? Why?

29. Do you have a favorite article of clothing? What? Why?

30. What is your strongest sense?

31. What is one guilty pleasure that you love too much to give up?

32. How many children did you say you wanted to have when you grew up? How many do you have?

33. Do you believe that you are selflessly selfish?

34. What makes you feel alive?

35. What are the simple things in life that you truly enjoy?

V

Leaping into a greater level of your life!

Write out your four year plan, whether it be business or personal. Write out each step that you need to take to reach each goal and cross them off as you accomplish them!!! When you have completed a goal. Start a new!

www.ingramcontent.com/pod-product-compliance
Lightning Source LLC
Chambersburg PA
CBHW080344300426
44110CB00019B/2502